University Press of Mississippi

[signature]

Eudora Welty

Seeing Black and White

by

Robert MacNeil

I feel quite unnecessary here.

In his foreword, Reynolds Price has said so many important things about Eudora Welty's pictures—and said them so beautifully—that not only do I feel my tongue tied, but my mind. Yet, I am so grateful to Mr. Price for introducing me to an observation by John Ruskin that I would like to repeat part of it:

Hundreds of people can talk for one who can think, and thousands can think for one who can see.

In Eudora Welty, we are faced with the one in hundreds who can think and the one in thousands who can see, and nothing proves the second part of that better than the book we are here to celebrate.

If someone had come upon this collection of photographs in an attic with no evidence of who took them, but was moved to guess (as I'm sure he would be) what would the photographs say about the person who took them?

The searcher would know that she was a woman because she has left the imprint of her own shadow, a ghost in the driveway leading to the haunting ruins of Windsor at Port Gibson, a feminine shadow, with a wide skirt and wings of hair.

But he might as well divine that the photographer was a woman because the subjects, particularly the female subjects, find her so unthreatening. They are not defensive with her; they remain in unguarded positions, like the languid woman in the cover photograph, "Saturday Off." They do not sense in her anything to make them strike attitudes, to strut or conceal. She puts their vanity at ease, she does not arouse their shame. She is someone who is permitted in moment after moment to share their humanity on their level, without pretenses.

That is a blessed quality, that ability to be received by strangers as they are, not feeling required to pose. Miss Welty says she never posed her subjects, but it is a rare person who does not make people feel they have to pose—to look happier than they feel, to look less sad, more optimistic, less defeated, to put some face on life—and a rare photographer who does not have to make people put on a show of being unposed. "Don't worry about me. Just do what you'd normally do," I have said, and I have heard said, hundreds of times by television news crews trying to capture people naturally, when the most unnatural thing in the world is happening to them.

Well, Miss Welty has an answer to that: she was fortunate to be in a time before self-consciousness set in. I think she is characteristically too modest. I am not sure there was such an age of innocence, before self-consciousness, before cameras were admitted to the Garden of Eden. I think Eudora Welty has the gift of making people unself-conscious.

The investigator searching the photographs for clues about the picture-taker might notice another quality: the absence of herself in the pictures. Henri Cartier-

Bresson said he took his pictures "wishing to be always the person seeing, never the person seen." That is clearly how Miss Welty worked, perhaps by design, probably by instinct. They are not photos of pieces of herself: they are not taken through a subjective lens or filter; they are not the gathered evidence for some angle on the world. They are not judgments and they are not editorials or propaganda, they are not studies in sociology. Hers is an objective lens.

It would be clear to the searcher that the attitude she brought to making these images is remarkably free of personal coloring. Yet she is not invisible to the subjects of her pictures. They are looking at someone. They are not staring opaquely, as people stare at police photographers; as they stare out from newspapers; as they gaze into the bottomless pools of their own ambition from their yearbooks; as they look smugly into the camera recording their promotion to branch manager; as they squint reluctantly against the sun of families determined to document happiness.

The people in this book do not think this woman with a camera is trying to take something away from them. You still run into people in some cultures, who believe that in taking their picture you are stealing something from them, some essence, some piece of their soul. And in the modern sense they may not be so wrong.

Photography in all its forms has made extremes of the human condition a valuable commodity. The news industry gambles on futures in the commodity of human suffering and spends lavishly to record it. Over land and ocean without rest thousands speed at the bidding of networks or newsmagazines to track down the most bloody, the most tragic, the most touching, most sentimental, most patriotic images they can find. And those images become our news, and increasingly our national memory and our history. To supply that commodity lives are risked, privacy is invaded, people are humiliated, or undressed: we are shocked, angered, titillated, embarrassed, and relieved that it is not we who stare so numbly at the world. In the end we are uneasy, because often the pictures come with an odor of exploitation. The person taking the pictures cares only to get an effective picture. He may be totally indifferent to the human condition he witnesses. Indeed if he is a professional he had better be indifferent, or he would be sick with the accumulated suffering he has witnessed.

The person who took these pictures is not indifferent: she is curious but affectionate. I think her pictures are acts of love. I don't mean personal love but the kind of encompassing love that some few people feel for their fellow humanity; a loving sensibility that is not blind to human folly, greed, cruelty—but witnesses it all compassionately.

Someone who studied these pictures carefully would know in what time and place they were taken. And if the investigator thought about that he might ask himself: why, back then, did she take so many pictures of blacks? Why did she? Blacks filled the landscape, of course. Yet for many whites, perhaps for the majority of whites, blacks were visible but invisible. But why go out of her way in the 1930s to take their pictures? It is difficult to say without sounding unctuous; but the answer must be that this photographer recognized blacks as human beings and the circumstances of their lives made her curious.

It is so easy for us to see it now half a century later, when our eyes have been forced open. Two little black girls carry little white dolls. The irony, the poignancy of that, shouts to us today. How many did it whisper to in Jackson in the '30s? Clearly to Miss Welty. We can see the pathos in the little black boy with his hopeless home-made kite and his aviator's helmet, but she saw it then.

Time magazine recently published a special edition celebrating 150 years of photojournalism. In an essay, Lance Morrow quotes Susan Sontag as saying that photography is an elegiac, nostalgic phenomenon. And he adds: "no one photographs the future. The instant that the photographer freezes is ever the past, ever receding." Well, sure, obviously: but is that the end of a photograph? I fancy that I see the blacks looking through Miss Welty's lens into the '60s and '70s. I wonder how many of those black Mississippians of the '30s will see these photographs—from the other side of history's looking-glass—and recognize themselves.

Photographs are not just of the past. Those that touch us become part of memory, they exist in our memory as well as on the wall or in the album or book. The picture of little John Kennedy saluting his father's coffin, the naked little girl in Vietnam running away from a napalm attack, any of our own children in their tender years exist on paper but coexist in our minds and grow with us, as all memory does, changed, as we are by time. As Miss Welty has written in *One Writer's Beginnings*, "Each of us is moving, changing with respect to others. As we discover we remember, remembering, we discover." I think in that sense she was photographing the future because the reality her pictures represent so unaffectedly was not to be endured. In that sense we have all moved, changed, with respect to others.

Unaffectedly: that is the thought I have been looking for. A sensitive investigator would conclude that these photographs were taken without affectation.

But what would he (I don't know why my investigator has to be he—but he is!) what would he conclude about the motives of the person who went out to take these pictures?

The *Time* essayist I quoted is talking of the photojournalist who is paid for sensation, who is hungry for Pulitzers, who has trained his eye and sensibility to filter out the mundane unless intended as ironic background to the sensational subject. The photojournalist is looking for the most extreme: poverty most wracking, horror most horrible, death most foul. That becomes competitive as the industry, with television leading, ratchets up the threshold of what is unusual, of what we can bear to look at, finally, of what we expect. We are becoming addicted to sensation: demanding ever more brutal fixes from our photographic pushers; more violence from places like El Salvador; more provocative eroticism as in the Robert Mapplethorpe photographs now causing such controversy; more extreme standards of feminine—or masculine— desirability in fashion photography. That has always been a way to catch the popular attention, "to split the ears of the groundlings," as Hamlet put it. That is increasingly the standards today's photographers have to match to be bought, to be printed, to get new assignments.

Miss Welty's photographs reveal a mind drunk with curiosity about the mundane. Our investigator would turn with relief to these images of ordinary truth, and realize, when he had decelerated to their speed, the person who took them had the gift of being fascinated by the usual.

Also the investigator, musing over the time and

place, might conclude that this woman was in her way confident and bold. It requires boldness to step out in public and take pictures of strangers. Much safer to take pictures of buildings, or trees, or people in crowds. To get close enough to take such intimate portraits demands courage as well as a disarming manner. You cannot be too shy; you have to push in there boldly. In fact you have to be quite pushy in a way that goes against the grain of people brought up as gentlefolk. You have to be willing to intrude on privacy, not to invade it, but forcefully to ask to be admitted to it. This gal, he would realize, was no shrinking violet.

Add to that Mississippi in the 1930s, a young white woman making herself conspicuous taking pictures of blacks in the streets of Jackson. Can you imagine what people said? "There's that Miss Eudora Welty with her camera again, taking pictures of nigrahs." They probably said a lot more than that. And, knowing precisely what they would be saying, our lady photographer must have had enough spirit to say to herself: "Well, I don't care what people think." Not easy in a small city to think that. Much easier to move your independence away, somewhere where it won't show so much.

Our investigator has exhausted his powers of deduction and goes over the evidence he has deduced, assembling the person who emerges.

A young woman (young he concludes after studying again the profile of the shadow in the driveway at Windsor), a young woman, with an independent mind and a bold spirit; but modest, unaffected and unthreatening in her demeanor; who puts strangers at their ease and makes them unself-conscious; who finds a world of fascination in the people and life around her; yet is herself worldly and well traveled. Above all he would conclude this is a person who looks on life with a loving and compassionate eye, and records it with a governing and fierce intelligence.

That is what this book reminds us about Eudora Welty. It throws into fresh relief the qualities that have made her one of the great writers of the twentieth century, the qualities that link her to the great writers of other centuries.

A largesse universal like the sun
(Her) liberal eye doth give to everyone.
Her largesse shines from this book.

Copyright © 1990 by the University Press
of Mississippi
All rights reserved
Manufactured in the United States of America
93 92 91 90   4 3 2 1
The paper in this book meets the guidelines for
permanence and durability of the Committee on
Production Guidelines for Book Longevity of the
Council on Library Resources.

Designed by John A. Langston

Library of Congress Cataloging-in-Publication Data

MacNeil, Robert, 1931-

   Eudora Welty: seeing black and white/by Robert
   MacNeil. p.   cm.
   ISBN 0-87805-471-5
   1. Welty, Eudora, 1909-   . 2. Photographers–
   Mississippi.
   I. Title.
   TR140.W43M33   1990
   770'.92--dc20
                           90-12640
                               CIP
British Library Cataloguing-in-Publication data
available

The repository for Eudora Welty's photographs is
the Mississippi Department of Archives and History
in Jackson.